A Poetic Attempt
at Being Feeble

Michael J. Ferris

First Edition: 2021
Rs. 200/-

Cyberwit.net
HIG 45 Kaushambi Kunj, Kalindipuram
Allahabad - 211011 (U.P.) India
http://www.cyberwit.net
Tel: +(91) 9415091004 +(91) (532) 2552257
E-mail: info@cyberwit.net

Printed at Repro India Limited.

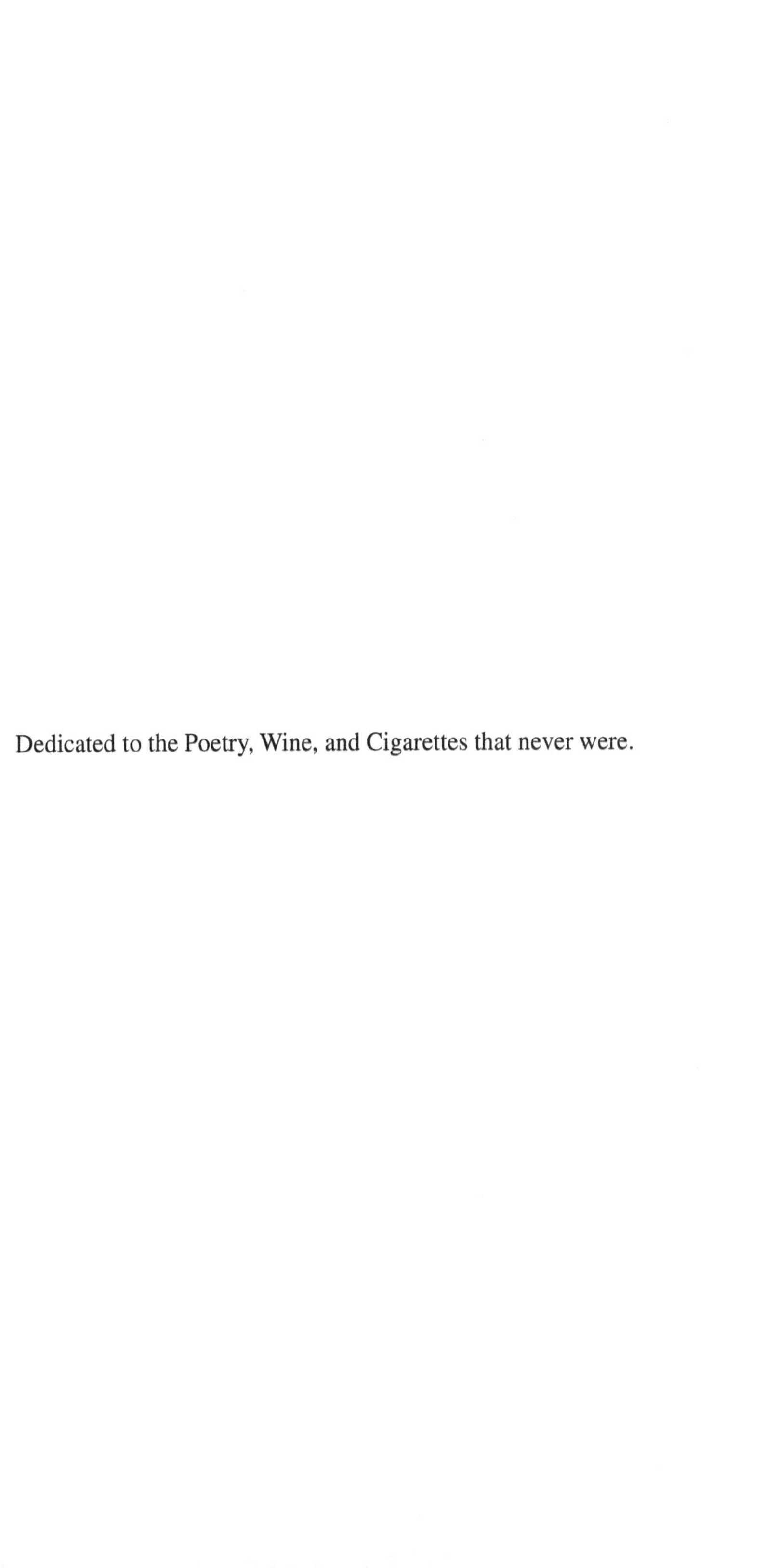

Dedicated to the Poetry, Wine, and Cigarettes that never were.

Acknowledgements:

For John Keats previously appeared in Voices From Here 2, published by The Paulinskill Poetry Project, 2017

Jackson Pollock Studio Tour previously appeared in Volume 4 of The Stillwater Review, published by The Betty June Silconas Poetry Center, 2014

Love Poem That Isn't previously appeared in Volume 6 of The Stillwater Review, published by The Betty June Silconas Poetry Center, 2016

Foreword

Winter, 2004: Hesitant and shy because I only expected to know one or two people at this gathering, I walked into the coffee shop. Used books lined the walls, interspersed with displays of specialty coffees, teas, teapots, and mugs. The space had a high ceiling but felt cozy, carved as it was into a section of an old stone building that had begun as a gristmill and then had been converted into a small theater. Throughout its history, this was a place of stories. On this Tuesday evening, the Grist Mill Café had stayed open late for the monthly meeting of a group of poets and writers.

A young man sat in the far back corner. His face glowed in the subdued light. He watched everything—I would learn that he always sat in that back corner, a spot from which he could observe all the action in the room. I don't know if someone introduced us that first night, but this was where I first met—and over the years got to know—Michael Ferris. He was a fixture at these First Tuesday events of the Writers' Roundtable, as well as at other poetry readings throughout northwestern New Jersey. I saw him often, because I, too, became a fixture at these events.

I begin with this personal anecdote because it contains the seeds of all that I love about Michael's poems. The sense of place evoked by my memories of First Tuesdays at the Grist Mill Café comes back in so many of the poems in this collection. Even readers who do not know specific locations such as Yetter's Diner, Lambertville, or Route 46 through the New Jersey city of Clifton will be able to picture similar places from their own experiences (and imaginations) and feel the visceral impact of such familiar scenes, sounds, scents:

Woke up smelling like
New Hope and your forgotten
stores of Ferry Street.

The poems in this collection draw on the duality of memory, the comforting and the haunting that often go hand-in-hand. "14 Maple" ends with the lament, "I am just a custodian of history. / You in Clove Hill Cemetery would know. / My dust is with you now." Readers will be transported by images in these poems, such as these from "Poem for My Father":

It made me think of my father walking by,
again,
on gyroscope hips as he looks for his coffee and Pall Malls,
his hands doodling on invisible paper.

We see in these poems a crossroads of influences, showing the poet's love of his craft and respect for the history of this art form. Perceptive readers will hear hints of the Beats whispering to the British Romantics. There are also allusions to music and visual arts. Michael Ferris's poetic voice, however, is never derivative. He is merely timeless.

The tone of these poems can be nostalgic, but it's never an easy nostalgia. A reader senses that a Michael Ferris poem—even one in past tense—is a prediction, a glimpse of the future. These poems gently suggest to us that time is not to be trusted. I return again and again to the short poem "Emmanuel, I'm Worried," drawn to its mysterious and poignant tone:

Emmanuel, I'm worried.
I see miles wearing the tires thin.
What was once pale Irish is now headstone gray.
Emmanuel, I'm worried.
You look deeper into the rear view mirror than I do, but I see more out the windshield.
Yet, you smile, and so do I.

I have known Michael Ferris now for seventeen years. Our paths have crossed at poetry readings, workshops, and poetry festivals, in coffee houses, art galleries, houses of worship, and colleges. Our local community of writers continues to grow and prosper and sustain. Or is this just another of the tricks of time in a poem by Michael Ferris? Was it just last week I found the courage to walk into that coffee shop in Andover, New Jersey, and wonder about everyone else who was there, everyone who seemed to belong and yet remain apart? Yes.

Jean LeBlanc

January, 2021

Newton, New Jersey

Contents

"Mike?" It started with
a strummed guitar chord, like what
Dave Mathews once played.

I once saw it rain
for forty days, forty nights.
This rain is nothing.

Lakeheads. Parrotheads.
Metalheads. Shitheads. They are
all the same to me.

Why weren't they ever
proud of me? Maybe I should
go sit on the tracks.

"What did I do?" "Why
did they hurt me?" Animals
and I need shelter.

It's simple; it's art
as a way of life, not life
as a way of art.

Scooter represents
freedom because my dreams were
all bought at wholesale.

Cloudy aurora
borealis was really
just light pollution.

It's quite amazing
at just how much can be said
with two syllables.

Woke up smelling like
New Hope and your forgotten
stores of Ferry Street.

Like a video
game; drop a quarter and so,
so easy to play.

I sat watching trains.
The clouds were nostalgic.
The trains not so much.

I'd gotten up close
to her today. Turns out she
is cute after all.

The car. Washed and waxed.
Fifth Highwayman. Challenger.
Us. In love. Again.

Shelf Life

Music and laughter.
Onomatopoeia of espresso exoskeletons,
and cappuccino prosthetics.
Sounds of pages turning,
friends aging,
and there's still no seat for me at the cool table.

October Rain

October rain tapped my skull for information I could not give.
I got in the car,
looked in the mirror,
and smiled;
not a hair was out of place.

Old Lion

I am the old lion lying under a shade tree,
roaring about past hunts,
conquests.
I miss my pride.
I am the old lion,
societal thorns in my paw,
National Geographic photographers hassling me,
waiting for death,
and watching the sun set over the Ferlinghetti plain.

Missing in McDonald's

Early morning,
empty place,
and dewy dirt clung to creosote.
My head bowed over a breakfast of cooling eggs,
weak tea,
unmeltable butter on rubbery hot cakes,
overly spicy sausage,
greasy hash browns,
a dry biscuit,
and two little cartons of milk to wash it all down.
McDonald's.
I'm lovin' it, but I should be loving you.

The Poem on the Wall

so much depends
upon

a poem on the
wall

slicked with some
polish

beside the waiting
commuters.

All Roads Lead to Breakfast

No Manhattan here.
Yetter's Diner.
A cranky waitress perfumed with chain-smoked Marlboro reds,
and wearing support stockings insists on calling me "Honey."
Good food.
Bad service.
Just how I like it.
Across a field I count blue cars heading south into Ross' Corner;
Destination: Irrelevant.
I thought about the yuppies in their white houses with white
interiors; a zit in need of popping on the skin of a manicured hill,
and their ceiling fan cooled kitchens where hyper teen daughters
and their hyper teen friends congregated.
They didn't care I roamed lawn and garden centers.
They didn't even know I hid on back roads, and drank lemonade.
Down the road, I floated over the hills, and into the Fairgrounds.
Music has forever colored that time.
These blue collars were there.
No Manhattan here.
Nor should there be.

Failure

I
stumbled
in the
scumbles,
and spent
days
in the
glaze
only to find out
passion
is a
has-been.

Art by Death

Urban parking lot.
Route 1.
Power lines connected summer's dots.
There was nowhere to be.
I couldn't go back to Manhattan; the island was in ruins, and inhabited by vampires.
I remembered when I sat up all night, and watched my lover while she slept.
That other one had snarled at me from across a table; she hated me for no good reason at all.
Frustrated, like Basquiat, I walked to the train station, and waited for the ghost train that would never arrive.
My fists full of Bop, I walked home noir-style through early morning Hopper streets, and past the long closed Automat.
When the bullet went through my brain, it created a Pollock.
The coroner's report read, "Cause of death: *Full Fathom Five.*"

Emmanuel, I'm Worried

Emmanuel, I'm worried.
I see miles wearing the tires thin.
What was once pale Irish is now headstone gray.
Emmanuel, I'm worried.
You look deeper into the rear view mirror than I do, but I see
more out the windshield.
Yet, you smile, and so do I.

Amy

I was changing channels for 11 seconds when our blushing
pilgrims slowly said grace that quiet,
cold,
and still night.
New softness explored,
my hand rested on the cashmere sweatered small of her back,
and I nuzzled her kitten-soft hair.
In our foreign nights,
we shared space,
heaving and sighing,
rising and falling,
and there were ships made of ribcages as she coyly bit her lower
lip and pinky tip before baring a lover's smile.
"I made a mess," she'd said.
The space between us was warm,
comfortable,
and grew the night Cupid took his arrow back.
I wanted to tell her how I felt, but the right angle of an L and the
point of a V had cut my tongue too deeply to speak.
All I wanted to tell her was how much I lo…
I'm bleeding again.

For Jean-Michel Basquiat

No ignorant art today, though there was some talk of an alterna-
tive to God, and something about Easter eggs.
This artsy afternoon finds me dipping my fan brush in synovial fluids.
On my couch,
the same couch from a dream where God had massaged my
shoulders to soothe me, and lightning had blued the way,
the same couch where I held a black and white painting of the
Eiffel Tower, it all makes sense;
it's the suckerpunch from childhood, and only now is the bruise visible.

Dinosaurs

I wasn't prepared for the rainy streets at night,
the strange quiet that comes with buying coffee on a Tuesday night,
or the effects of Time's scorched earth policy.
"Someday, you're going to inherit this," he'd said.
We're dinosaurs now, my egg the last to crack.
Our years were spent with philistine raptors attacking us,
anti-intellectual t-rexes taking bites from our sides,
and pop culture pterodactyls shitting on us.
From here,
in the back of the line,
I can see the herd isn't kicking up as much dust as it once did.
It's moving slower,
lumbering along with hands arthritic from years of editing and rewrites,
and starting to thin out.
I dread the day when the last sound heard will be the echo of the
dark being turned on,
and our conversations being turned off.
Someday,
if we're lucky,
a curious archaeologist will dig our bones,
and read our gloriously wordy fossils that begin with Page 1.

A Day in the Life

Talk.
Don't talk.
There's so much to say.
Wake to mornings filled with humor and haze.
Go through the day only to find the stench of burial masquerading as a kiss.
Impenetrable wall of roses; red one side, yellow the other, and a pocket full of black petals.
Smear.
Teasing makes the fangs grow sharper.
Drink in front of my dancing serpentine baby.
Leave with bloody, perfumed stained fingers.
Night leers over, and torment begins.
Broken hearts and loneliness want to spend time.
Spilled glass of wine.
Gleaming knife smile.
Sleep.
Dream of falling backwards off a monument, and a raven-haired angel.
Wake.
Talk.
Don't talk.
There's so little to say.

Things can only get Better

It was a lie I liked believing,
a walking staccato,
like Tom Waits after a long night.
At night,
there were trumpets over a lost battlefield,
and blurred bridges.
It was the dream to awaken my world,
a scented autumn remembered,
affluence hoped for,
and I never left the living room.

The Real Thing

In the young night's silence, the fireflies were oddly absent.
From the deck, I watched the slow procession of clouds float by
as the sky made its gentle transition from pink to gray to purple to
blue to black.
Spiders were having a party in the Japanese maple, and spraying
me with webbing while I wished I could sit on the front steps,
drink orange soda,
and watch the sky burn.
In the gray of the newly mown lawn, I could see the grayer
shape of one the cats walking slowly.
There was no Lambertville.
There is no new hope.
No brush could paint this.

Urban(e)

There was talk that warm afternoon, something about owed money, lawyers, and problems with Optimum and Verizon. I wasn't there, though; I was on the deck listening to a passing train.

That night, I'd find myself watching TV. On the screen was the face of a recently killed teen from East Orange. On the radio, hip-hoppers had shouted at me to text something to someone.

Now I have the grim prospect of listening to the radio while lying in my bed on a Friday morning, or walking along 34th and Something on a cold night while I wished I were home watching Britcoms. Was it always this way?

I remembered sitting in my Aunt Mary's kitchen on Forest Place in Rochelle Park, and watching U68 station promos with that giant record dropping onto the Empire State Building's needle-like antenna and spin. Lunch was in the backyard, and I needed something to do.

On Saturday mornings, after Goya commercials and bike rides, past Frank Malatesta Moving and Storage in Paterson, through the park in Saddle Brook, along the railroad tracks, under bridges, and in the weeds where a discarded pornograph spun at 69, there was The City; The City where black men in purple shirts and camo pants had worked in the back of trucks, The City where metallic banners hung over car washes on the West Side by the River, The City of Channel 4, The City of Billy Joel and John Lennon, The City I never found.

At night, there were car rides over summer streets, Shannon let the music play, and I pondered the opening of Video Music Box. As it turned out, Eddie was crazy, and Nobody Beats The Wiz because The Wiz had beaten us.

There is Beauty Here

There is beauty here on this shore.
I have congress with pines, and grief counseling with a cypress.
One tree had even volunteered to be turned into paper for me to
write a love letter that would never be read,
poem understood,
or a list for groceries that would be shopped for alone.
The trees will throw their ticks on me, and my fed-upon blood
will be introduced to animals as they take it somewhere.
When I die, I will be buried in a winter hill overlooking a warm
and softly dozing town,
like a cinnamon roll and coffee.
The trees will be happy to have their silence back.

Music of the Last Days

You were there with me then under cottony tundra,
and my compass was useless.
After the scenery had blurred,
and cups emptied,
I walked,
dazed,
along 33rd towards 6th,
and remembered how the choruses battled.
Walking up the steps from the subway and into the heated shade
of the sidewalk in Union Square,
the keyboards were low air conditioning.
I know I mean nothing to you,
and that's okay;
you don't mean a thing to me, either.

Maybe the Gray

Across the field, I see the copse of trees of starting to shake its
leaves off now that the nights have cooled,
and autumn is setting in.
There were times,
smiles and laughs,
dead parents,
making love in a hammock,
and Christmas
that I have heard about and might write about someday,
as they did,
as my bootsoles get inked from walking through their penstrokes.
Gray,
one shade away from Death,
is on them,
in me.
Maybe the gray's not so bad.
After all, we were young once, too.

Poem for my Father

He smelled of death,
like a parent in mourning,
like Uncle Chris in that picture, the one with the green couch and
white blinds,
like the way my father had mourned having me as his son.
It made me think of my father walking by,
again,
on gyroscope hips as he looks for his coffee and Pall Malls,
his hands doodling on invisible paper.
In his second childhood, he plays in the streets of
misremembered Montreal where he finds abandoned houses with
broken windows,
crumbling plaster,
unfamiliar names,
and forgotten faces in distressed frames.
On his good days, he watches the Phoebe Snow pull into the
Broad Street station,
eats pbj sandwiches for lunch in Military Park,
and the undiagnosed shellshock keeps the quad 50s firing well
into the night.
In that night,
Jazz wails,
neon flashes,
dinner is at the Automat,
(.10 sandwich, .5 glass of milk, .5 slice of cherry pie, .5 cup of
coffee)
Bacardi fades,
dew clings to sharkskin,
and Hemingway is a nightcap.

There is a long night coming.
One of his favorite songs is *What a Wonderful World*.
Maybe it was, even if just for a little while.

Conversely

By the bridge, the mayflies were an atomic dust cloud in the dirty
fallout of neon windows.
Inside, we discussed if amputation was
change,
removal,
alteration,
or separation.
On the way home, rotund spiders had descended from the eaves
over the windows, and were slowly eating the mayflies from the
inside out.

Crash

The pictures of innocence are
faded,
dated,
and sticky with years of cigarette smoke and indifference.
Anywhere but here.
The talk in traffic on 7th.
The espresso in your eyes, and the marble on your tongue.
The kiss on the corner that lit the Chrysler Building.
The sigh by the Lake.
You didn't tell me where the road turns.

Hold Your Breath

So, it's come to this.
The morning ritual of airing rooms, and brooding by the picture
window.
Channels strobe by;
DNA results,
hoarders,
and 90s nostalgia.
Afternoon shadows stretch long.
I meditate on Billy Joel from 30 years ago,
and James Karen's Pathmark commercials from my childhood.
Saturday nights,
after dinner,
during Britcoms,
Millie is still alive.
In my head, I roam the old house.
It is empty,
like the boxes over my shoulder waiting for memories to be
neatly folded and put in them,
and taken out of this house,
one by one;
a death march of living.

Tarpaper Meditation

Bob Ross said to work in layers.
In the background is the Manhattan skyline.
boom box rising,
Whodini's *FiveMinutes of Funk* playing,
a possible soundtrack from that time we went to explore the
abandoned tb hospital on Staten Island.
In front of that are trains going back and forth,
carriage returns of life's stories being written in rolling stock.
In front of that are frustrated drivers on Route 280,
some remembering the horseradish from Passovers of youth.
In the foreground,
down the block,
at the corner,
in the weeds,
casings the cops didn't find from last week's drive-by.
Below me, a sign reads, "Apartments available."

South Main

Dust in the canal house.
Somewhere,
unbalanced antiques in a shop.
Across the street, books are made love to as the young mind
screams out for more.
Old-fashioned sodas on the counter.
Acrobats go by on motorcycles, and the street clears.
Lilacs above the Canal over the street where I once brooded.
A woman,
my type,
passes me,
but doesn't notice.
Black,
moving east,
with trailing blue.
A life remembered from a bench.

Love Poem that Isn't

My eyes are pretty.
That's what you said, anyway.
Why did we do it;
all those walks from Gramercy Park under a sweaty moon and
grimy streetlights,
the dusky blue bedroom thoughts.
In Penn Station,
I smelled your hair as we hugged.
and you looked at me just a little longer.
On our respective rides home,
you'd worry about me,
and the lights in the meadowlands would blur again.
This poem is not about you.

For John Keats

Because of her,
I binged on Eve of St. Agnes,
Ode to a Grecian Urn,
To Autumn,
and, of course, Bright Star.
I read them all, and had wondered what it was like to sweep the
dead butterflies out of the bedroom.
I forget the words now.
Your death was not in vain, John.
Ask Fanny at the bottom of the stairs, when she's standing; she'll
tell you.
I'd written your name in the water, and pondered it as my finger
had dried in the still air.

Still Cuts You Up

I still think of you in those nights when I hear something close to
cobalt blue,
you,
dark,
cool,
wet for me as I walked your leaf-scabbed streets,
and brooded on your corners.
A streetlight, (You know the one.)
God's winking eye under starlines waiting to be framed.
Oil memories drying,
and acrylic memories forming.
Charcoal quotes.
I remembered the sensuality of sculpture,
appraising glances,
caressing hands over curves and texture.
A moment in a dream.
A long walk back to the car to drive home, and awaken.
I still hold the secret close.

Forgive Me

The lights returned to your old house before they did to mine.
Through the trees, I saw lights on in the kitchen,
the kitchen where we snacked,
and there was a faint glow coming from the room where we
played Mermaid.
I thought about when we sat under the cherry blossom,
and I thought it was confetti in our hair.
I'm sorry, Kristen.
I'm sorry I was your first broken heart,
and had misplaced your innocence.
I should've been your first, but not like that.
I'm sorry the mermaid died alone on an empty beach,
and that the dorsal fin on the shark was mine.
I'm sorry that your eyes that once looked upon me with love
looked at me with hate.
On summer nights,
the crickets don't tell the whole story.
I'm not the same boy I used to be.
I hope the wind in your arms kept you warm.
There's a fence around the yard now.

Haunted

I don't know why, but the rain is heavy,
oppressive,
and leaves my clothing hanging and pointed like a Kubert draw-
ing as I walk past a cemetery of thought.
Parties last until 4 a.m.,
and I restlessly sleep in rattled chains.
Someone short-sheets the bed,
and leaves me short changed.
Come morning,
she is gone,
and I have to clean ice crystals from the lint trap.
I am at an intersection as a zombie conga line passes,
and see the faces of those who have crossed my shores.
This bite isn't going to get any better.

Blue 10 A.M.

I think of Clifton with its thin traffic on Route 46,
quiet diners,
voices of party girls evaporated yesterday morning,
and the City's skyline,
standing,
with arms folded.
Who's home now?
What are they watching?
I wonder how many cell calls they'll sneak on Browertown Road later.
They will shout it out.
My dreaming brain stands under a bridge,
looks at the years of wear and tear,
looks at where the Erie ran,
wonders what trains when through and what was being carried,
turns up its blue collar,
thrusts its hands into empty pockets,
and walks on.

After You've Gone

I could still smell you in the sheets.
I saw where your head was on the pillow,
the silhouette in your body glitter,
and I remembered that way your foot arched and slid over a
black satin glacier.
Beside the bed is a black and white picture of you that will turn sepia,
then crumble into forgotten history.
I remembered the ghostly sleeve of sheer white curtains tickling
my skin as I wandered your forest,
and dreamed wearily outside the walls of your perfumed garden.
A breeze came in,
and I smelled the cool water of Gaian musk as a thunderstorm
had soaked her thighs.
The sheets will be washed,
dried,
folded,
and put away only to be replaced by new ones.
Mountains would be replaced,
and windows closed and locked against a bruising autumn.
I'd smooth out the new creases and folds,
I'd remember you,
and you would forget the color of the satin,
and me.

Across Town

I can tell you this now.
In those sleepless and hysterical nights,
I'd look east in my bedroom.
The spinning party light's four suits left dream warrior gashes in
the postered sheetrock.
I wondered what you were doing,
if you were alone,
and had hoped you were on your bed while thinking about me.
I should've known better than to let you go alone through the chorus,
reverb,
and delay.
Was this...
Well, maybe.
Just a little.

Picture

Gray afternoon.

Basquiat's water tower over the Salvation Army shield.

Artsy girl always on her blue period.

Brian Eno through the windows.

Acoustic guitar in the living room.

Pastel fingers clutching a coffee cup.

Black tights in August.

Passion on the landing.

Sullen silence across the living room.

Art supplies, suitcases, and a fern when she left.

What I Miss

What I miss most are our nights,
drives north along the River,
Alternative music,
and coffee on a quiet Route 27.
There was that way the tiki torches were lit,
the party lights glowed,
and gunpowder mixed with dewey grass after we shopped at Big
Lots.
I cursed the light pollution spilling down from Manhattan turning
black to pink,
and I'd hear those words,
"Brooklyn calling."
"Brooklyn calling."
No one.
Ever.
Answered.

Another Sunday

Bone on bone has started.
I walk alone on a cold North Main Street,
wish I were in the cozy comfort of oil heat,
and remember the lonely glow of Christmas lights in a sweaty
window.
The street is mine, and mine alone.
I know what every day is like,
and they're all silent and gray.
I would share greased tea with you,
but the tea shop closed down many years ago.

Jackson Pollock Studio Tour

All I can do is show you how he works.
The smoked cigarettes were thoughts,
and brushes a way to express.
The canvas is a thrown hope that you will understand,
and the box is for boss sides, daddy.
I can't tell you how he saw the rhythm.
The drips on the floor were a mistake,
but the art was not.

Fallout

There's rain on the window at the back of the bus,
a wish made on a bad penny and thrown into the drowning pool,
and a disco ball spinning over an empty dance floor.
Aimless drive 90 miles outside Chicago.
Alone in the laundromat folding the sweater you gently gave me.
I drove past here 97 times tonight.
I roamed the room,
and watched the water spin down the drain.
I traced your lipstick stain on the glass,
kissed where your lips were one last time,
and carefully cleaned it.
The moon had distracted me from my art.
In an abandoned warehouse,
a band played in the murk.
I heard.
You didn't listen.

Veronika

"Can I call you 'Mickey,'" she asked me.

"Only if I can call you 'Mal," I answered.

"I love you, Mickey."

"I love you, Mal."

So far from that time,

that time when we threw dreams from rooftops,

and declared ourselves the King and Queen of St. Mark's Place.

Days spent in French elegance,

and nights spent when I licked your backseams.

You wondered if your black lipstick would ever come off me,

and we joked about being kicked off Caligula's party list.

It was so quiet the night you left.

The subways weren't running,

and I was the only one in the station.

I see your ghost standing in the fields along Route 15.

The pumpkins are rotting in the field,

and the apples have been shaken to their seedless cores.

14 Maple

We were better in black and white,
those days when we smoked pipes on the bench in front of the
barber shop.
those days when the trains still ran.
At night, we sat on the porch in a honeysuckle cloud,
and we talked about the Farm and Horse Show.
We were friendly,
folksy.
It's all color now.
The bench is gone, and the barber died years ago.
I linger in antique shops like slow roast coffee,
ask what was,
and no one has answers.
I own nothing;
I am just a custodian of history.
You in Clove Hill Cemetery would know.
My dust is with you now.

Alessandra

Her name was a dream whispered on the corner of 34th and
Something.
Our nights began with counting stars,
talking about nothing all night,
memorizing the curves of each other's bodies,
and blushing dinners.
We progressed to Manhattan sunrises,
midnightish train rides,
and coffee on the corner.
It all ended the night the crickets stopped chirping.
The seat next to me is cold,
unoccupied.
It could've been different. It *should've* been different, it says to me.
"I know," I answer.
I turn my head,
and wait for my stop.

Stranded

There's a picture of us talking that day.
Do you remember?
On a street with the ghosts of Book Row who
flipped out
flipped off
flipped pages.
You took an interest in me.
We talked about Gershwin,
Porter,
Kern,
and two others I can't remember.
You wondered if I listened to them,
and I wondered about the summers of your youth in Coney
Island.
We didn't exchange names;
tipped hats were enough.
I watched you walk towards St. Mark's Place, and wanted to
hear your stories of the Automat,
Chock Full O'Nuts.
By now, I imagine you answered God's call on a candlestick
phone.
I hope the walk up the gold dust was an easy one.

Words of the Road

"If you ain't turnin', you ain't earnin'"

"TA Petro. Full service means at your service."

There are those words again in my pre-dawn darkened bedroom,
the words of when I'd drive to Ohio for fireworks and back in a day,
260 air conditioning,
New Radicals playing just right at the right time,
and exits to places I'd never see.
When I saw the Sapp Bros. Coffee sign, I wondered where I
could get a cup.
At rest stops, there were weary couples.
In the lobbies, there were people looking for something, anything,
to read,
appraising eyes,
and always someone checking the bottom of their cup of instant
coffee from the vending machine to see if they won the card game.
I sat on a bench,
snacked,
and watched the world go by.
The Penn DoT channel on the TV in the lobby was calling for
severe thunderstorms.
There are those words again,
words that pull me off Airport Road in Allentown as a hawk
screeches on my radio,
pulls me down to Trexlertown,
back up Route 78 to Hellertown,
Phillipsburg,
words that call me home.

Seduction Between

Lovers in a suburban afternoon.
A commuter train passed by outside the window, and the room
smelled crisp.
There was that way she talked to me through a smile, and her
manicured hand caressed my hand like it was an antique about to
be bought.
She asked if I remembered when the world was open, big, and exciting.
I didn't.
My world was a burned out husk, a leftover from that night when
a lit oil lamp was kicked over and the wheat field silently burned.
I trembled, she kissed, and beating butterfly wings warmed my stomach.
She had to remind me to breathe.
I remember the sound of the kiss; a white wooden window being
closed against a hot and urgent thunderstorm.
We settled back, and her fingers roamed my leg like lost and
careful explorers.
The windows shuddered against impending musk.
The rustle of cotton.
Words caught between pages.
Poems yet to be written.

Silence

There was quiet when Jane sold shoes,
like the slow fade that came with drinking hot cocoa while
waiting for the afternoon's UPS delivery near Christmas.
I watched the lightning over the mountain, but the rain would
never come.
On the deck, I drank mandarin orange iced tea, and listened to
the shock of moth hearts stopping.
Around me, the cicadas counted
1…
2…
3…
and held their breaths.

Digital Nights

Digital nights preceded by analog days,
the way we sounded running through the streets of Coney Island,
cherry pie of the underworld on the 18th floor of the Hotel
Pennsylvania,
baby Lain under the duvet on summer nights,
the firestarter in Powder Mill Curve,
Godspeed gray,
the halcyon cloud that hung over Manhattan,
blue studio air conditioning in the intersection of 32nd and 7th,
walking off a long night of invisible wounds in Penn Station,
numb noses in bathroom stalls,
1 minute and 59 seconds in Barnes and Noble,
remembering at the top of the escalator,
Stamina Rose on Blackwell Street,
strong in love in the Meadowlands, (Say it again.)
trinity on Bay Street,
the youth of the nation in denim jackets in the Manhattan Mall,
watching the Midnight Express pull away;
nights like these weren't meant to end, nor were they meant to begin.

Poetriptych

I. Opening Act
Fleshy curtains closed, opened, and closed again.
Outside, the rain timpanied the roof, and I waited until she drove
away so I could touch my lips, just to be sure, without her seeing.
SHE kissed ME.
I touched my lips again, and savored the muscle memory of her
being there.
On the ride home, there were shoulder rattling chills as the
butterflies had swarmed, and took off in one direction.

II. 39 Going on 16
The halls and rooms were new, yet familiar.
I remembered square dancing in the gym classes of my child-
hood, marveled at how alien a new hand felt, and wanted the
dance to last just a little longer.
I remembered.
In older days, we aimlessly drove country backroads, she fed me
Boo Berry out of the box, and I was bulletproof again.
That song played again, I blushed, and she smiled.

III, After Ice Cream and Rainbows
What do I do now that the cream in the ice cream has soured,
and the rainbow and burning sky we chased has been replaced
by low hanging storm clouds?
Nature walks in dead forests are too long now, the apple trees at
Masker Orchards are in the gray frost of a black winter, and only
the bumblebees by the Rose of Sharon talk to me now. I look up
the hill from Plant Street, and see where love's steam whistle
blew. The butterflies never flew again.

Sundays

Here's where the story ends.

Then, a walk past indifferent Indian corn that ended in a coronal blast of glass, white, and chrome.

Things had cooled at night, and dew clung to grass for dear life.

I found myself driving past a well-manicured lawn with a house where an upstairs bedroom was vacated by a Swatch wearing, R.E.M. listening art student.

A Replacements poster was left behind.

Outside, a pumpkin was so orange the leaves were jealous, and fell from shame.

Past that, playful children ran, and they were lucky. They went shopping in Chester, and had gotten to be upmarket, even if just for a few hours.

Now, there is no more corn, and the coronal blast has left me blind. The nights are still cool, the pumpkin long rotted, and Chester is just drive-through territory.

Here's where the story begins.

9 789388 319775